MW01592407

A COLLECTION OF POEMS

Gabriel Vitalone

A publication of

Eber & Wein Publishing

Pennsylvania

A Collection of Poems

Copyright © 2015 by Gabriel Vitalone

Library of Congress
Cataloging in Publication Data

ISBN 978-1-60880-392-7

Proudly manufactured in the United States of America by

Eber & Wein Publishing

Pennsylvania

Dedicated to Evelyn,
my wife of sixty years,
truly the wind beneath my wings—
Chris, Peter, Nancy and her husband Mark,
my children who have filled my life with joy—
and Ava and Emma,
my granddaughters
who complete our circle of love

Contents

The Wind

One night while in my lonely room,
I heard the wind's familiar tune.
It made me think that it was true
You're much alike, the wind and you.

I listened closely to its song,
It stayed a while and then was gone.
Before departing it said to me,
"I crave excitement, so I must flee."

In mighty gusts it blew away,
'Tis then I heard my sad heart say,
"We can't be friends for long it seems,
For winds depart as quick as dreams."

I told my heart not to despair
That even wind must rest somewhere.
Its blustery gales to zephyrs turn
And soothe the heart where true love burns.

And so my heart and I will wait
Till the wind we love will meet its fate.
Excitement gone and craving rest,
It returns to the one who loves her best.

WRITTEN FOR EVELYN
FEB 1952

The Aged Athlete

When old men were young they were just like you.
They played the games and ran and hit and threw.

They lived as though their skills were ever owned
But passing time took back what nature loaned.

Yet deep inside the memories still remain,
Of golden moments in exciting games.

On city lots or stadium fields—
The joy returns the skills seem real.

So when you meet a body frail and wrinkled face,
Remember to look beyond this time and place.

And see within the old man's eye
A younger man with spirits high.

Then listen to this survivor's song
And marvel at the courage of the strong.

The games we played have come and gone
But the game of life continues on.

No medals or trophies to be won
We still play hard till life is done.

On Modesty

In days of yore when athletes scored
Or made a super play,
They may have smiled but in a while
They quickly turned away.

They left acclaim to those who watch
And cheer the player's deed
But took no part in self-acclaim
For this there was no need.

Today there is a newer way
Whenever one plays well.
Attract attention to the deed,
Self-glory is the sell.

But sport reflects life, and life has changed,
And it is plain to see
The most important thing today
Is me, me, me.

Let's say a prayer for modesty,
That it might soon return.
For the humble shall be exalted,
As the exalted will come to learn.

Veteran's Day

When a soldier faces death he prays
That this bitter cup might pass away
And he might live another day
He fights.
Although he wages someone else's war
To bring the peace he's yearning for
As it was done so many times before
He fights.
And when a soldier dies, I cry
For when a soldier dies, I die
And when I see his face, I sigh
It is I.

An Old Man's Lament

What has happened to my world?
Where has all the goodness gone?
Another day, another dawn
Filled again with gaping yawns.

Wars persist and innocents die
We are left to wonder why.
Rich get richer, poor descend,
Ask the muse when will it end?

Government "of" and "by" and "for"
Broken by greed, democracy no more.
The world is not a better place
Than when I entered time and space.
Gadgets galore, it's easier—know
That weakness prevails as selfishness grows.

I pray that others will make it change
So that I will not have lived in vain.

Getting Old

I know which way the road will go,
I cannot change it though I know.
I must not falter in my task,
To keep my courage is all I ask.

I owe to those who love me well,
To live with verve and not rebel.
Though aging is a weakening thing,
It can be fought, take time to sing.

Our attitude can keep us whole
And nurture the eternal soul.

Memorial Day

Soldier brave, where have you gone?
No longer here to walk the lawn—
Or smell the flowers by the stream.
No longer here to dream the dream.

No longer in your mother's gaze,
No longer hearing your father's praise.
But you are in a better place
Where noble heroes have their space.

And though you're gone
Behind life's door,
Know that you are
Remembered evermore.

The Teacher

For who am I that I should say
These things to others who may pass my way?
What message do I dare to give?
What lesson's rule should I obey?
Look but inside yourself and find
A part of universal truth.
We are indeed alike in kind
In search of who we are
And how we grew.
The answer that we seek
Cannot be bought
Nor does it lie in others
Or in things
Reach for your soul
With kindly measured thoughts,
Touch it and your life will sing

Brothers and Sisters

Brothers and sisters—a strange game,
So much is different, so much the same.
With mother and father a family is made
With caring and sharing the strange game is played.
Add giving and taking, laughter and tears
And a feeling of closeness, which lasts through the years.
Give thanks for your father and thanks for your mother.
They gave you the gift of a sister or brother.

To Peter

We glued each golden dot to the bedroom ceiling
According to the celestial map.
In the dark, the constellations glowed.
The galaxy was in your room.
It was ours.
Easy to ponder the universe,
Easy to dream.

The Old Coach

The dream is over
It was lived well
It's well remembered
And still enjoyed

The Body

The human body, able and strong,
Performing its tasks all life long.

Muscle and bone and deep inside,
Organs which tend to mystify.

Arms and legs will carry us far
And help to make us who we are.

But wonder of wonders is the brain.
Without it, all would be in vain.

Victory

Have you ever watched a tree
Fighting with the wind?
The odds are against it,
The foe is strong.
Attacking gusts bend the tree
As if to break its spine
But when the wind stops to catch its breath,
The tree springs back.

So the battle is waged
Until the wearied wind
Moves on to other trees
In other places.

And what is victory for the tree?
It gained no prize
It did not have before.
But its success means that it stands
To face another wind.
Today's prize is tomorrow.

Hope

Sadness can't bring you happiness
So smile as you go on your way
For life is at best an enigma
And work will determine your play.

Count all of the blessings that fill you
As you suffer your hardship and pain
For it's only despair that can kill you
While hope is the food for the sane.

On Aging

The day will come when you will see another man
With whitened hair and wrinkled face.
The day will come when you will see another man
With body bent and slackened pace.

But be not fooled by what appears to be
For sameness is often greater than change.
What was remains for you to see
And covers now an even greater range.

The heart that beats is still as full of love
And feelings go beyond the pitied fears.
The runner as he ran both far and near
Still runs inside ignoring passing years.

Mandela

Nelson Mandela is gone
He leaves a gaping hole
How do we replace him?
How can we match his soul?

Let us review what he taught us
About courage and freedom and rights.
Pursuing justice in prison
Through endless days and nights.

He left us his poignant message
As what was the best way to live.
Give up your freedom to gain it,
When there is nothing else to give.

Lost Love

Lonesome roads and dreary days
Saddened friends along the way
How to face them, what to say
Remember the good

Plans that crumble, goals postponed
No one knows you, you're alone
Dreams not followed are seeds unsown
Remember the good

Counting blessings seems so trite
How can counting shorten night?
Can we store a ray of light?
Remember the good

Think of family, friends and song
As you question right from wrong
All must battle, all life long
Remember the good

Seasons

Against the background of the woods
The leaves fall one at a time
The first messengers of the end of summer
Too soon the trees will be bare
And there is a certain sadness
The eventual snow, yet to come, brings hope
And out of the beauty of hope
The joy of spring arrives
And the leaves return

The Mountain

My room faces a mountain
Close and steep
The first thing I see
When I wake from my sleep

Behold nature's beauty
Silent and strong
Symbolizing life's
Continuous song

Aging prevents
My physical ascent
But climbing it is
My natural bent

I find that
If I close my eyes
I feel like I'm climbing
To the sky

The mountain of course
Will never change
But I can climb it
In my brain

The Gift of Forgiveness

When the sun goes down on your anger
Morning brings no relief
The fermentation of anger
Brings us nothing but grief

It is time to forgive those who grieved you
So reach deeply into your heart
For the gift you thought you were giving
Is a gift to yourself from the start

The Poor

Why else do we enrich the rich
While others are in need
Who struggle vainly to survive
While viewing other's greed?

We blame them for their status
Though fate has not been kind.
We say it's all their making
And pay them little mind.

So think of all your blessings
That made you so unpoor,
And think of those who helped you
When you were so unsure.

Perhaps someday we all will learn
There is a better way
Let us care and share our bounty
So the poor will have their day.

Vacations

Vacations are a wonderful thing
Consider the joy that they may bring
With places to go and planes to fly
Or ships that take us far and wide
They give us a view of city and town
Or mountains and lakes
Where beauty abounds

We go away strangers
And as we roam
We learn so much more
Than staying at home

When we learn from others
Different from we
We know how the world
Was intended to be

.

My Grandchildren

Where did their childhood go?
Was it not yesterday that they were small?
My how they grow—
Remember when they held my hand
So not to fall?

But that was then
And then must make some room for now.
I must let go,
Let nature do its share
To shape the sprouting boughs.

But I'll be near
In case I'm needed in my role.
I still have much to give
To those who touched my soul.

Words

They say I have a way with words
I really don't know what this means
I merely say the way I feel
Somehow the words describe the scene
And if the words communicate
The deeper feelings I possess
I hope they bring a message true
To help you in your loneliness

Children

It has been said the child is
father of the man
And mother too—no also—ran.
The world we know would long be gone
If all as children had not been born.

Through trial and error, joy and pain
They weave a life that's not in vain.
We watch them grow and day by day
We also grow—come what may.

The day will come when they are grown
And we are left with memories sown.
They live in us and we in them,
They are the flowers, we are the stem.

As we grow old, have children near,
They give us hope and calm our fears.

A Tree

Look at me
I am a tree
I am here
For you to see

What do I have
To say to you?
Stand up tall,
Be straight and true.

Lift up your arms
And reach to the sky
Wave to the birds
As they go by.

Give shade from the sun
And cool to the night.
And with the wind whisper
That all is right.

Joyce Kilmer knew,
It's plain to see—
Fools write the poems,
God makes the tree

Growing Up

Not all our memories are good,
At times we did some foolish things.
We did the things because we could,
With little thought of what the future brings.

But memories are persistent and they stay
And point the folly of our former way.
We live a better life today
When we remember the errors of yesterday.

Old Songs

Some of us remember the old songs
And some are even sung
But mostly they are forgotten
Like a bell no longer rung.

To those of us who sing them
One thing is very clear,
There is no song like an old song
To help us shed a tear.

Dream

A dream dances on the threshold of reality
It is a whisper in an unknown tongue.
We seek the message it hides
And the search is as intriguing as the dream.

Autumn

The days of August slowly slip away.
The mountains and the shore
Are memories new,
But be not sad.
For autumn brings its own joys
With colors bright
And chilly nights
And then—the holiday delights.
Enjoy each day.

Course #11463

I gave you a grade but I have not judged you.
What you have learned, I do not know.
Ask yourself some pointed questions
Where did I start from, where did I go?

What did I follow, was it outside me?
What did I follow, was it within?
Where did it lead me, what did I find there?
Did I pursue it or merely begin?

Each day as a teacher
You must face your students
What will you tell them?
What will you say?
How much will you give in your effort to serve them?
For as you have given,
They give the same way.

The Poet

The poet's eyes can see the source,
The soul that makes things what they are.
The poet's ears can hear words unspoken
Or whispered softly from afar.

The poet's mind can never sleep,
It wrestles hard with the thoughts that burn.
The poet's heart is full and deep,
With feelings shared
Without return.

Potpourri

Cold water…
On my face…
In the morning.
Awake—alive
Bring on the day

The best wrinkles in my face
Are those that came from smiles.
Smiles may go,
But the wrinkles remain,
Symbols of what was,
What is, and what will be.

When love is not enough
Then greed has won.

Those who take more than they give
Steal from their own happiness

I am the runner
I am the race
I am the prize

Hope Too

Evening comes with lengthening shadows
Announcing the end of another day.
Soon the darkness is upon us
Worrying those who've lost their way.

Sounds of night will reassure us,
In the distance a train whistle blows.
Bringing hope from those who miss us,
As each star above us knows.

Mom Is Dying

Why can't I cry?
Can grief be true without
The tears?
She has to die—
Consider the travail of
Ninety-six years.
But how she lived!
She lived the life that
Others ought.
She lived to give,
Denying to herself
What others sought.
Yes, she must die—
But dying will not change
What she has done.
A glowing life—
There is no doubt that
Heaven's won.

New York

Faces—they are the city.
Universal images etched on
A canvas street
Blurred in a sea of movement
Going everywhere
Going nowhere
At home here.

New York II

City walk,
Look up,
Above the shops and stores
To the place where people live.
Rows of windows,
Some open
Some shut
Like a row of uneven teeth.
Curtains and shades
And occasional pillows on the sill,
Comfort for the surveyors of the scene.
Recorders of those who come and go.
Flowers in window boxes.
Better than neon.
Music competing with street noise
Serenading life above the ground floor.

Family

Mother, father, sister, brother,
Grandma, grandpa, uncles, aunts,
Where did this thing called family come from?
Was it luck or was it chance?

Perhaps a higher power planned it
To show the world how to share
The blessings that are all around us
Through the love from those who care.

Then and Now

Then was then, now is now,
Then was why, now is how.
Now is spend, then was save,
Now is do it, then—behave.
Then was we, now is me,
Then was easier to agree.
Then was simple, now diverse
Which is better, which is worse?
Then was better, but then is gone,
We must do better for those yet born.

The Professor

The campus sings a silent song
Of students gone.
The setting sun smiles
As it smiled before on deeds and dreams of the young
Reminding us that though years may pass
Youth really stays the same
And all they need is love
And work, God's help and mine.

Reminiscence

Thoughts of the past
From younger years
When dreams were new
And still believed.
Of struggles and separations,
Joys and sorrows,
But always friends.
Bridges across time binding us
To the best of the past.
Soothing our purpose,
Kindling our understanding
And giving our lives a touch
Of immortality—
For whatever lives in the heart
Lives forever.

Response to Dylan Thomas

You cannot hear my silent rage,
I really do not want to go.
I love this place of joy and tears
To go a place I do not know.
I pray there is a better world
Beyond the bounds of space and time
And as I slide the slippery slope
To find it ends in perfect rhyme.

CPSIA information can be obtained at www.ICGtesting.com
Printed in the USA
BVOW08s0405201115

427557BV00001B/2/P